Comfort Edwin Barrows

# The Development of Baptist Principles in Rhode Island

From 1636 to 1875

Comfort Edwin Barrows

**The Development of Baptist Principles in Rhode Island**
*From 1636 to 1875*

ISBN/EAN: 9783337379766

Printed in Europe, USA, Canada, Australia, Japan

Cover: Foto ©ninafisch / pixelio.de

More available books at **www.hansebooks.com**

# THE

# DEVELOPMENT

OF

# BAPTIST PRINCIPLES

IN

# RHODE ISLAND.

## 1636-1875.

## A DISCOURSE

DELIVERED ON THE OCCASION OF THE SEMI-CENTENNIAL ANNIVERSARY OF
THE RHODE ISLAND BAPTIST STATE CONVENTION,
AT PROVIDENCE, MAY 12, 1875.

BY

## REV. C. E. BARROWS,

*PASTOR OF THE FIRST BAPTIST CHURCH, NEWPORT.*

*PROVIDENCE :*
J. A. & R. A. REID, PRINTERS.
1875.

# HISTORICAL DISCOURSE.

In the year 1636, in the opening Spring, a small company of men made a settlement within the borders of the present State of Rhode Island. They were but a handful in number, poor in worldly possessions, outcasts indeed from the society of civilized men, and they constructed for themselves but the rudest dwellings in the unbroken wilderness. The event, so inauspicious apparently in its beginnings, has, however, proved to be one of the most memorable, not only in American history, but in the annals of the world. For here was inaugurated a government on an entirely new basis, embracing principles hitherto unknown or unrecognized in the polity of nations.

Though now for the first time incorporated into a civil constitution, the principles themselves were as old as Christianity. Baptist principles may indeed be traced through all the Christian centuries from the beginning. They furnish a history—yet to be written—parallel with that of the Papal hierarchy, which too early acquired an almost absolute supremacy over the religious thinking of Europe. They appeared in the rise of the Donatists in the fourth century, of the Waldenses in the twelfth, of the Hussites in Bohemia who heralded the Reformation in the sixteenth. They were potent among the people of England from the time of Wickliffe to that of the Commonwealth. But watched with jealous care these principles were constantly smothered, and wherever one bolder than his fellows arose to proclaim them, his voice was instantly hushed in martyrdom.

Our task is not, however, to discover the origin of these principles, nor to show their divine authority, nor to follow them in their earlier manifestations, but to indicate how they have been developed here within the limits of this small State. Thus circumscribed, the theme is so large that it must be imperfectly treated in a single discourse. The history of the development of Baptist principles in Rhode Island, covers the beginnings in this country of a large and influential body of Christians, as well as the formation of a civil State. For, as Massachusetts was settled by Congregationalists, Maryland by Roman Catholics, Pennsylvania by Quakers, and Virginia by Episcopalians, so Rhode Island was settled chiefly by Baptists, whose principles gave shape to its government, and direction to its subsequent history. Here Baptists for the first time in the history of the world, were permitted to have a controlling influence in the framing of a civil government, and here their earliest churches in this new world were formed. Here, then, we have the practical outcome of their doctrines, in regard both to the state and the church. Here their principles appear in absolutely new conditions, are brought to the test of actual experiment. With the settlement of this State begins very naturally a new chapter in our ecclesiastical history.

## STATEMENT OF PRINCIPLES.

Before proceeeding to discuss their development, it may be well to call to mind what some of these principles are. The one that will first occur to almost every mind is that of liberty, religious and civil, with which the early history of this State is intimately and most honorably connected, for whose sake indeed the State was first settled and its government organized. This doctrine enters as the corner-stone into the very foundation of the Commonwealth, and reappears in every part of the beautiful and symmetrical superstructure. But this primary truth, so grand and sublime, and at the same time so simple and self-evident, does not stand alone, in solitary grandeur, and unrelated to other truths. It forms a part, and a necessary part, of a system. A brief statement of them will, we think, show that Baptist principles are so correlated as together to form a complex unity, a self-consistent whole. While in our present review, we shall have specially to do with the forms in which Christianity embodies itself rather than with its essential doctrines, there can be no satisfactory treatment of the former, without at least an incidental reference to the latter, since the latter determines the former. The Baptist conception of the church, grows out of the Baptist conception of Christianity itself. That which separates Baptists from Christians of other names, is not simply the quantity of water used in baptism—the difference is deeper and more fundamental in its nature.

Baptist principles may be regarded as falling into four divisions : Those pertaining, first, to the individual considered alone, and in his personal relations to God ; secondly, to the formation of Christian churches ; thirdly, to the mutual relation of churches ; and fourthly, to the relation which churches sustain to civil society and the world.

A primary truth in the kingdom of Christ is the personal nature of his religion. God addresses men personally. He lifts up and clothes with solemn dignity the individual. Every one stands in direct relations to his Maker, and is personally responsible to him. No human being can come in between a soul and its God. No one has a right to attempt to mediate. No one may dare with impunity to enter the sanctuary which belongs to God alone. Hence the doctrine of soul liberty ; of the inalienable, the indefeasible right of private judgment; of the right of every person to examine for himself the word of God—man's authoritative rule of faith and practice, to form his own opinion as to the requirements it lays upon him, and to act upon his own convictions of duty. In the matter of religion every one must act for himself, must for himself repent of sin and believe on the Lord Jesus,—must become a new creature in Christ. This doctrine of a new life in Christ Jesus is a cardinal truth, and one that must not be obscured ; one which, if we mistake not, the Lord has sought to preserve alive in the minds of men, by the very forms in which he has clothed it.

This new life takes on a body adapted to its use, is the informing principle of the Christian church, determines its constitution,—that it shall be composed only of re-generate persons, or, in Scripture language, of "living stones," of those who have been touched into life by the Spirit of God. The organization is the simplest pos-sible, its function being to conserve and express the spiritual life of the members. When that life is faint, then the organization is feeble; if that life dies, the organization expires; but when the informing life is healthy and active, then the church is mighty, overcom-ing all its foes. The members of a church compose a brotherhood, each one being subject directly to Christ, the Head of the church and its Lawgiver. Every separate church is in government a unique republic, executing by the voice of the brotherhood the ordained laws. Hence the independence of the churches of all extraneous hu-man authority, in managing their internal affairs. The church organization must not obscure, but express the doctrine of the personal responsibility of each member to Christ, and that his life is derived from personal union with him. This same spiritual fact—the new life of the members—determines also both the subjects and the form of the ordinances, which are symbols of the new life. None are proper subjects of baptism but such as have had this experience, have entered into possession of this new life,—only believers in Christ, such as can make profession of personal faith. And the form—as a symbol—must set forth this new life, this life from death. And this experience of the soul—this death to sin and life to holiness—is connected with the death and resurrection of Christ. Hence the beautiful and expressive rite, the burial with Christ in the liquid grave and the rising with him to newness of life. Only once is a believer baptized, as only once does he enter into life; while the maintenance of this life by Christ, who is himself the bread on which it feeds, is brought visibly and symbolically to mind at the memorial table on which are placed the bread and wine—emblems of the broken body and shed blood,—the partaking of which is often repeated. The order, therefore, in which the ordinances stand is significant; the order is indeed divine, and the two ordinances form together one whole. When thus scrupulously observed they bear eloquent testimony to the truth, and shed light upon the way of salvation.

While churches are in their internal government independent of all outward control, they are not isolated bodies. They hold peculiar relations to all bodies similarly constituted, that have precisely the same conditions of membership, and are subject to precisely the same code of laws, and acknowledge allegiance to one and the same Lord. By virtue of their common relationship to Christ and his law, they are one in the truth, members of a single family, form a sisterhood—are one body indeed of which Christ is the Head. There must be consequent fellowship and community of interests, and corresponding obligations and duties.

The relation of churches to civil society and the world is two-fold. First, it is one of jealous separation: the state having no voice in the management of the churches, to prescribe to them laws or to deprive them of their

privileges ; and the churches, as such, having no control
in civil affairs.  Secondly, it is one of mutual service:
the state throwing the shield of its protection over the
churches ; and the churches inculcating the great lessons
of virtue and integrity on which alone a republic may
rest, and keeping before the minds of the people their
higher obligations to God and his laws.

## These Principles in the Settlement of the State.

Having thus given in briefest outline a statement of
Baptist principles, we are prepared to trace their history,
which, even with external restraints removed, was not
entirely free and uninterrupted in its course.

The men who first settled this State were twice refugees.
From the relentless persecutions in England they fled,
with thousands of earnest souls, to this new world, for
rest and safety, only to meet with bitter disappointment.
For in the colonies they encountered laws equally
obnoxious, were subjected to an espionage quite as annoy-
ing, and fell under the displeasure of rulers who would
tolerate no dissentients from the established faith ; and
they were finally driven away, out into the further wilderness to find a home among the savages of the forest.

The New England colonies were planted by men eminent for piety, willing for the sake of their religion to
brave the hardships of pioneer life.  And those of the
Massachusetts Bay were second to no others in devotion
to religion and zeal for their faith.  Solicitous for the
honor of God and the maintenance of a pure church,
they had nevertheless by infant baptism incorporated
into that church an unholy and corrupting element, and
they sought to build up the church by the use of pro-
fane means.  The Puritans were not opposed to the union
of church and state, if only the alliance were made with
the true church—with their own.  Immediately on their
arrival at the Bay they established their religion, making

Puritanism the state religion of the settlement.* They sought here "freedom to worship God," but they were unwilling to grant equal freedom of worship to others. All dwelling among them must conform, and whoever dared to hesitate must be forced into conformity, not by Scripture and reason, by argument and persuasion, but by the strong arm of civil power. Hence, as heavy penalties were visited upon dissentients in the new world as in the old, the early history of Massachusetts Bay being a repetition of English history of the same period. While zealously guarding against the earliest approaches of error, and summarily chastising those venturing to differ from the authorized standards, the rulers found it impossible to secure absolute uniformity. Men would think for themselves, would study the Bible, and form their own opinions of its teachings. New and startling theories were being constantly broached. A large share of the official service was, as the records show, expended in fruitless efforts to regulate religion.

For persisting to entertain opinions of his own, Roger Williams was esteemed a dangerous man. He claimed the privilege to examine the fundamental principles of both church and state. He questioned the colony's right under the king's patent, and denied the authority of the magistrate to enforce the laws of the first table ; that is, the first four commands of the decalogue, as these refer solely to man's relations to his Maker. And finally, for his bold defence of the liberty of speech and of his right to discuss the questions of government and

---

* The Pilgrim colony of Plymouth must be distinguished from the Puritan colony of the Massachusetts Bay, which was commenced at Salem in 1628, and two years later, in 1630, enlarged by a settlement at Boston. The planters of the latter colony, though Non-Conformists, had never separated from the English Establishment : they believed in a national church. Hubbard, History New England. Mass. Hist. Coll. 2d Ser. V. 100, 117. The first comers to Salem entered into a solemn covenant with God and one another, "And because they foresaw that this wilderness might be looked upon as a place of liberty, and therefore might in time be troubled with erroneous spirits, therefore they did put in one article into the confession of faith, on purpose, about the duty and power of the magistrate in matters of religion." Morton, New England's Memorial. pp. 145, 146. Cf. Genesis of the New England Churches, by Leonard Bacon, pp. 462-468.

religion, he was banished from the colony. * Referring
to the opinions held by him which justified his banishment, his antagonist in a prolonged controversy, John
Cotton, says: "Under pretence of maintaining liberty
of conscience, purity of conscience is violated and out-
raged. † Before leaving England, Williams had come
into contact with the Baptists and been made familiar
with their articles of belief. ‡ By them he had been
taught many fundamental truths respecting the kingdom
of Christ, and suscipion was early awakened that he
cherished "principles of rigid separation and tending to
Anabaptistry." § Seed thoughts were producing their
appropriate fruit, were working out their logical results ;
for, three years after his settlement at Providence, in
March, 1639, ‖ he and a few others were baptized and
formed themselves into a church.

We are informed that there were Baptists among the
first settlers of Massachusetts Bay. "Infant Baptism,"
says Cotton Mather, ¶ "hath been scrupled by multitudes
in our days, who have been in other points most worthy
Christians, and as holy, watchful, faithful and heavenly
people as, perhaps, any in the world ; some few of these

---

* See Williams's own statement of the causes of his banishment—*Mr. Cotton's Letter examined and answered*, p. 41., *Nar. Club, Pub.*, I., 325 ; also Gov. Winthrop's account, *Hist. N. E.*, I.,
162.; Morton's *Memorial p.* 152.; Arnold *Hist. R. I.*, I., 41. Yet Dr. Palfrey ventures to
assert, that, "The sound and generous principles of a perfect freedom of conscience can
scarcely be shown to have been involved in this dispute," which led to his banishment. *Hist.
N. E.*, I., 413.

† Thus Cotton and Williams, the two disputants, agree in their testimony, and confirm the
statements of Winthrop and Morton. *Cotton's Answer to Williams* , *Nar. Club, Pub.*, II., 24.

‡ Williams says in his *Hireling Ministry, None of Christ's*, London, 1652, p. 11: "Amongst
so many instances dead and living, to the everlasting praise of Christ Jesus, and of His Holy
Spirit, breathing and blessing where he listeth, I cannot but with honorable testimony remember that eminent Christian witness and prophet of Christ, even the despised yet beloved
Samuel Howe." Quoted by Dr. Hague in his *Historical Discourse*, Providence, 1839, who explains : "A Baptist minister and pastor of a church in London, the excellent Samuel Howe,
successor to John Cann, author of the marginal references to the Bible," pp. 37, 38. Crosby,
*History English Baptists*, I., 164. Palfrey, *Hist. N. E.*, I., 414.

§ Morton, *Memorial*, pp. 151, 152.

‖ Winthrop, *Hist. N. E.*, I., 293.; Arnold, *Hist. R. I.*, I., 107.

¶ *Magnalia*, II., 459.

people have been among the planters of New England from the beginning." Though Baptists in sentiment, they had never seen their way clear to take a decided stand for the truth, willing to remain silent on the points in which they differed from the establishment. Others, like Hanserd Knollys and John Clarke * demanded the privilege both to hold and to express their own convictions. They insisted upon full liberty of thought and worship, and since this was denied them, they determined to depart out of the province. The former went to Piscataqua, and the latter, in the Spring of 1638, took up his abode on Aquidneck, now the island of Rhode Island. A meeting house was at once built and a church gathered.† This body was doubtless of a mixed character, but it soon gave way to a distinctively Baptist church. Thus the State of Rhode Island took its rise from two centres, one at the North and the other at the South.

## The Government Formed—Separation of Church from State.

It had been a standing reproach against the Baptists in the mother country, and repeated in the colonies, that they denied all magistracy, and would destroy all civil government; that, if they did not themselves hold these opinions, their principles necessarily gravitated toward both civil and religious disintegration. The term Anabaptist had become a synonymn for anarchist. Because they earnestly protested against the ecclesiastical functions claimed by the state, their opponents persisted

---

* Mr. Clarke is said to have "received his baptism in Elder Stillwell's church, in London." *Baptist Succession*, by D. B. Ray, Lexington, Ky. Clarke was certainly never a member of John Cotton's church in Boston, nor was he involved in the Antinomian controversy which so seriously rent that church, though he suffered on account of it, being disarmed, with many others, by the magistrates. *Mass. Col. Rec.*, I., 212. He arrived at Boston the first time in November, 1637, and, because the Summer had been extremely hot, went almost immediately to the north, perhaps to Piscataqua. The severity of the Winter, however, compelled him to seek a milder climate, and early in March, 1638, he settled at Aquidneck. *Ill. News*, 4 *Mass. Hist. Coll.*, II., 23.

† Callender, *Hist. Disc.* p. 116; Winthrop, I., 297, 328.

in the accusation that they labored for the overthrow of all religion, and the utter destruction of all civil authority. In vain was the charge repelled, and their belief in civil government most solemnly asseverated. Now, however, they were permitted by a most notable act to disprove the false allegation. In their settlements on the Narragansett shores, they constituted at once a civil government, and placed themselves under civil rule. At Providence, it was agreed that the inhabitants should yield "active and passive obedience" to this sovereignty "only in civil things."* On the island a more regular government was organized ; and, as though to disarm as far as possible all adverse criticism by rival and hostile colonies, and to assure themselves and all future comers that the State, though denied jurisdiction in the spiritual realm, was nevertheless clothed with divine sanctions, they declared that God was the source of civil authority, and his revealed will, so far as it pertained to the conduct of man with man, should be the fundamental law to govern in civil relations.† Thus while denying to it ecclesiastical rule, they claimed for the State authority to make and enforce laws, an authority delegated by God and recognized by His Word.

The separation of church from state was the distinctive feature of their government, the feature upon which they specially insisted, and which led the surrounding colonies' to regard their settlements with aversion and alarm. With sublime faith the first planters refused to establish any religion, or even to make provision for the maintenance of any—with sublime faith, we say, for the refusal was dictated by no unfriendliness to religion, since they were "Puritans of the highest form ;"‡ but by the belief that the religion of Jesus had power in itself §

---

* *R. I. Col. Rec.*, I., 14.

† *R. I. Col. Rec.*, I., 52.; *Baptist Quarterly*, Vol. VI., 483.

‡ Callender, p. 116.

§ "Truth is strong next to the Almighty. She needs no policies or stratagems or licensings to make her victorious." *Areopagitica.*

and required only moral and spiritual agencies for its support and propagation. They believed that religion had no need, even if it were possible, to call to its assistance the strong arm of civil power; that the propagation of the Christian religion transcended the might of the state; that hence within the sphere of the spiritual, secular authority had no right to venture. It was therefore not toleration our fathers claimed for themselves and would have accorded to others—it was liberty. To entertain their own religious opinions and obey their own religious convictions was not a boon they craved, but a right they demanded. Other governments had occasionally been indulgent, and tolerated a diversity of religious beliefs; but our fathers affirmed that civil government had no prerogative in the matter; that belief and worship were subjects wholly outside and above its jurisdiction. Here, within their settlements, all men of whatever faith could find refuge. The law-abiding were by their government protected irrespective of religious belief. In effecting this divorcement between the two realms—the civil and the ecclesiastical—our fathers were certainly making an experiment, were for the first time bringing long-cherished principles to the test. They nevertheless moved forward with assurance, believing the principle of separation to be right, to be supported by the word of God, and that his truth could not lead them astray.

It is of importance to remember, as the fact tells upon the subsequent history, that in their government our fathers sought for themselves no advantage not equally shared by all. Whatever they demanded for themselves they demanded also for others. They insisted that the privileges accorded to one religious body should be accorded to all, of whatever faith. What, then, it may be inquired, did they secure for themselves by their government? All they had ever asked for; not a theocracy, not a monopoly either of authority or of privileges—

simply equality before the law and an open field for all.
It was never their purpose to inaugurate a Baptist government, but a government in which Baptists could be
untrammelled and free, and their principles have a fair
chance in the world of thought and opinion. It was
simply an opportunity they desired, not an advantage
over their opponents,—an opportunity to defend their
tenets and make them known. They demanded that
principles—the true and the false—should meet in a free
encounter and determine which should stand,—that truth
might grapple with error and vanquish it. Liberty was
desired not so much for its own sake, not as an end in
itself, but as the necessary condition of an ulterior and
higher good.

While excluding religion from the functions of the
state, the founders of this Commonwealth evidently regarded it chiefly as a refuge for Christian people fleeing
from persecution, an asylum for consciences distressed
on account of religion, as appears from the concluding
words of their earliest code of laws: "And otherwise
than thus what is herein forbidden, all men may walk as
their consciences persuade them, every one in the name
of his God. And let the saints of the Most High walk
in this Colony without molestation, in the name of
the Jehovah, their God, forever and ever." * No con-
structive treason against the state was to be feared, no
inquisition into private opinions, no disturbance for religious acts.

The separation made in the colony had a twofold effect ;
it both relieved the church of magisterial interference,
and devolved upon her the responsibility of her own maintenance. The voluntary principle was, as a matter of

---

* R. I. Col. Rec., I., 190. "In her code of laws we read for the first time since Christianity ascended the throne of the Cæsars, that conscience should be free, and men should not
be punished for worshipping as they were persuaded, he required, a declaration which, to the
honor of Rhode Island, she has never departed from." Judge Story, Centennial Discourse,
Salem, 1828, p. 57.

course, assured to the church of Christ. If the state had no right to dictate rules and regulations to the church, then the church had no right to expect material support from the state. The church must make provision for herself. Voluntaryism, then regarded with so much suspicion, is now the system adopted by all denominations of Christians throughout the United States, as it must of necessity be wherever the separation between church and state has been effected; and the serious discussion of this system has, within the past few years, been strongly agitating the religious public of England.

New questions touching the relation of church and state are constantly arising. Some of these are even now engaging the earnest attention of many of our best thinkers. Those presented when the government was formed, though numerous and perplexing, were generally solved wisely and well. There were in the Colony those who held that civil government contravened their personal liberty. Their confused ideas it was not easy to clarify, though the attempt was made once and again. Civil government, said John Clarke,* must not lay its hand of power on "the hidden part of man, to wit, his spirit, mind, and conscience;" "its end is the preservation of itself, the whole and every particular part, and person belonging thereunto, safe in their person, name, and estate, from him and them that would rise up visibly to oppress and wrong them in the same." And Roger Williams in one of his letters, † likens the state to a ship at sea having many hundred souls on board, "pagans and protestants, Jews and Turks." While the commander may not compel any one to come to the ship's prayers, he may and must enforce upon all justice and sobriety, and command help from all either in person or in purse for the common weal.

* *Ill News*; 4 *Mass., Hist. Coll.*, II., 5, 6.
† Backus, *History*, second edition, I., 257; *Nar. Club. Pub.*, VI., 278.

. 3

## Further Remarks on Liberty—the Idea and its Limitations.

By their sober teaching and substantial government our fathers proved conclusively, that they held no wild and visionary notions concerning liberty. What they so earnestly contended for, and so resolutely sought in this new world, was exemption from civil liabilities on account of private opinions and acts of worship. They demanded that thought should be free, speculation free, and activity free, so far as the latter did not interfere with the rights and liberties of others ; in short, they demanded for all men the largest possible personal freedom. Theirs was not, however, be it remembered, a struggle for "free thought," but for freedom of thought. While protesting against the ecclesiastical authority of the state, and the authority of the traditional teaching of the church, they "yet reposed implicitly on an outward authority revealed in the sacred books of Holy Scripture, and restricted the exercise of freedom within the limits prescribed by this authority."

In later discussions the doctrine of liberty has often degenerated into something quite unlike that enunciated when this State was founded. We may further remark, therefore, that the liberty which we have inherited from our fathers, and which is the corner-stone and glory of our State, is not inconsistent with the absolute submission of the reason to authority, when that authority properly authenticates itself. In the late debates that have arisen concerning the meaning of the Vatican decrees, the Papists are right in saying that "there is an absolute necessity of some teaching power for man that can rise superior to the aberrations of human thought," but altogether and fundamentally wrong when that power is supposed to be vested in the Pope, or in the church, or even in an ecumenical council, and not in the sacred Scriptures, the production of men who spoke and wrote as the Spirit gave them utterance. This liberty is, indeed, far enough removed from that claimed by the modern rationalist who insists on investing the reason with supreme authority in matters of religion and subjecting to its tests the profoundest revelations of the Word, though he pretend to be a lineal descendant of Williams and Luther and Arnold of Brescia, of the long line of bold spirits who have been the defenders of freedom of thought. This being true, it certainly follows that the liberty of which we are speaking is consistent with positive beliefs, with the systematic statement of these beliefs, and with the carrying out of these beliefs into practical life.

Positive convictions respecting the utterances of the Divine Authority and unswerving fidelity to these convictions are in no way incompatible with this liberty. This does by no means require that one shall abide in doubt and uncertainty, be ever learning and never come to a knowledge of the truth ; that all questions shall be kept open, and none be considered closed and placed beyond dispute. While free in its search after truth, the mind is none the less free when, upon evidence offered, it settles down to a fixed belief. Definiteness of belief neither impairs one's own mental freedom, nor renders him intolerant of others' differences. A man with sharply defined views of truth is not thereby rendered either narrow or uncharitable, but may be distinguished even for breadth of thought and catholicity of spirit. Mr. Stuart Mill very justly considers the world under great obligations to earnest Christians for this inestimable boon. Liberty has a Christian descent, as history attests. Through Christianity, or rather through those who have apprehended the spiritual nature of the religion of Christ, has this blessing been transmitted to the world. Yet this is true, Mr. Mill explains, by a sort of happy inconsistency on their part.

"So natural to mankind," he says, * "is intolerance in whatever they really care about, that religious freedom has hardly anywhere been practically realized, except where religious indifference, which dislikes to have its peace disturbed by theological quarrels, has added its weight to the scales." Mr. Mill evidently studied Christianity as it is exhibited in state churches. It will not be denied that the fathers of this colony held truth tenaciously, with sharp and definite outlines, and with consequent positiveness, and yet it was liberty of thought and of speech of which they were the special champions.

Although the making of creed-statements, if for the purpose of governing the life, has sometimes been condemned even by good men, as opposed to the free spirit of the denomination, especially in this State, few surely will venture to assert that the formulating of truth is inimical to the right of private judgment. While resting belief simply and solely on the Bible, our fathers did not hesitate to make creed-statements, to draw up articles of faith, to put in systematic form the doctrines of Scripture. They recognized also "the importance of a true and proper science of theology," to be built up "out of the matter of revelation." Creed-statements are not inconsistent with the traditional doctrines of the State upon liberty of conscience. † Since there is in Christendom such a variety of beliefs, such contradictory ones forsooth, articles of faith are a necessity. Every church, indeed, has its creed, either written or unwritten,

---

* *Essay on Liberty*, p. 20, seq.

† As is sometimes affirmed. Some of the earliest fathers, as John Clarke and Obadiah Holmes, left confessions of their faith. Backus, *History*, I., 182-4, 206-9; and at a later period John Comer, transcribed into the *First Newport Church Records*. Confessions of faith have been intimately connected with the historical development of the Baptists. The Baptists of England issued, in 1643, an authorized statement of their belief; and another more elaborate one in 1677, which generally bears the date of 1689. Dr. Cutting says: "I think we were the earliest of the dissenting bodies of England in the issuing of confessions." *Historical Vindications*, pp. 85-106.

and all who seek admission are presumed to be in accord-
ance with that creed, in harmony with the belief of the
church.

When belief is thus translated into act, there is no in-
fringement of liberty,—of any one's liberty. A church
adopting certain articles as expressing its convictions
on essential doctrines, and separating itself from those
who do not subscribe to the same confession of faith,
does thereby trench on no one's private rights, touch no
one's inner life. Membership in a church is voluntary,
never compulsory. The constitution of a church must
not be confounded with that of a state. This remark
would be superfluous, if men of intelligence even did
not persist in likening the action of a church in with-
drawing from doctrinal dissentients, to that of the Puritans in banishing Roger Williams from their jurisdiction. In the very act of contending for the broadest
liberty of thought and of worship, our fathers claimed
for themselves the right to separate from those whose
opinions they deemed inimical to the truth, or subver-
sive of scripture teaching. They strongly insisted on
their right thus to withdraw. This was their liberty.
The right to separate from the Establishment, to protest
against its corruptions, was in England a principal issue
involved in the long and sanguinary struggles of the
seventeenth century. It is well to remind ourselves that
this was the very end sought in the earnest conflicts of
that period for liberty. For the sake of this right Puritans came to New England. For exercising the same
right our fathers were driven to this State. Before his
banishment Roger Williams had affirmed * that "he
durst not officiate to an unseparated people." And John
Clarke, arguing for a pure church, said† "that by preaching men were to be made disciples before they were to be

* *Letter to John Cotton, Nar. Club Pub.*, VI., 356.

† *Ill News, 4 Mass. Hist. Coll.*, II., 14.

baptized, and then taught to observe all things which Christ had commanded for the order of His house; for they and they only that gladly received the word of salvation by Jesus Christ were baptized; and they and all they were joined to the church, and continued in fellowship and breaking of bread and prayers."

## Controversies Respecting the Church—Quakerism, the "Six Principles," Doctrines.

One of the questions which in that period convulsed English society and in large measure shaped English politics, pertained to the nature and functions of the Christian church. Similar discussions disturbed the peace of the colonies. Some of these discussions, indeed, first appeared here and afterward in the mother country. In our present historical survey we have to notice several ecclesiastical controversies, some of them continuing through many years, and bitter, perhaps, in their spirit, as was the character of the polemics of the age.

The earliest religious controversy in this State of which we have any account, indeed arising almost immediately after the settlement, involved two fundamental questions, namely, the sufficiency of the Scriptures as a rule of faith and practice, and the existence upon earth of a visible church with visible ordinances. There were those on the island who, as early as 1640, pushing still further the principles of the "Antinomians," went beyond the written word and claimed to be in possession of an inner life, of a revelation from the Spirit supplementary to that of the Bible.* They also maintained

---

* See in this connection a brief analysis of the tests of truth employed as ultimate, with an examination of the advantages and dangers arising when these tests—sensation, intuition, feeling—are respectively applied to religion as the standard of appeal, in Farrar's *Critical History of Free Thought*, p. 25, seq. "If the feelings be relied upon as the sole arbiters, especially if they be linked with the imagination instead of the intuition, they may conduct to mysticism and superstition by the very vividness of their perception of the supernatural." The mysticism of the Quakers of the seventeenth century is of this character." Ibid. p. 20. Cf. Lecky, *History of Rationalism*, II., 84.

"that there were no churches since those founded by
the apostles and evangelists, nor could any be, nor any
pastors ordained, nor seals administered but by such,
and that the church was to want these all the time she
continued in the wilderness, as yet she was." Others
went so far as to teach * that "man has no power nor
will in himself, but as he is acted by God ; and seeing
that God filled all things, nothing could be or move but
by him."

As these persons professed to be seeking more light
than they had, including a fresh revelation from heaven,
they were denominated *Seekers*. Roger Williams had
the preceeding year, a few months after his baptism,
himself become a Seeker.† There were many such earnest inquirers in England ‡ and the older colonies. After
diligent search among the wrecks of that time for the
true church they concluded that it was impossible to
find it, and began to entertain the opinion that, since the
church was lost in the general corruption, there must
be a new beginning, with new apostles to reinstitute the
ordinances and worship of the Lord's house. § The chain
of succession had been broken. A few ventured even to
deny that any external church or visible ordinances had
been divinely furnished, and to teach that both the church
and its ordinances are to be understood in a purely
spiritual sense. And still others, under this cover, fell
away from religion altogether. Two obvious truths
were neglected by these men seeking for light. First,
that they were to build churches after the model given
them in the New Testament, that here is the sure light

---

* Winthrop, II., 38-41.; Backus, I., 97.

† *Scott's Letter, in George Fox's Answer to Williams*, 1677, p. 247; Backus, I., 89.

‡ Crosby, *Hist. Eng. Bap.*, II., 294 seq.

§ The subject of succession—"Apostolic " or " Baptist "—troubled not a few who were find-
ing their way into the light. "That the power of religious ministers is derived by an external
succession from the apostles, through the churches of Rome and England" was, very naturally
the belief of many of the Puritans. It was later the belief of such men as Drs. Stiles and
Hopkins. Backus, II., 312, 368.

to guide them in the midst of the deepest darkness; and, secondly, that any church observing the order herein indicated is in direct line of succession from the apostolic churches—that for a spiritual church, though organized and possessing rites, the true succession is a spiritual one.

This must be the class of men—these Seekers—Mr. Clarke has in mind when he bids men remember that "the spirit that does not exalt Christ cannot be the Spirit of Christ, or the Holy Spirit of promise; and urges them to try the spirits, to bring them to the wholesome words of the holy apostles, prophets, and the Son of God; and counsels that it be the Christian's care to search the Scriptures, and THEREIN to wait for the power and glory of the Spirit of God." He also charges the people to steer clear of both Scylla and Charybdis, of the opinion of those on the one hand who destroyd the purity and spirituality of the church by uniting it with the civil power, and by introducing into it unregenerate material by infant baptism; and of the opinion of those on the other hand who denied that there were any visible churches. He would have them avoid both extremes; "not turn to the left side in a visible way of worship, indeed, but such as was neither appointed by Christ, nor yet practised by those who first trusted in Him; nor to the right in no visible way of worship, or order at all, either pretending....that the church is now in the wilderness, or that the time of its recovery is not yet, or else pretending that God is a Spirit, and will in spirit be worshipped, and not in this place or in that, in this way or that." * Thus, while maintaining the spiritual constitution of the church, he adhered to its outward form, its organic structure, and put honor upon the Scriptures, teaching, with Chillingworth, that "the Bible, the Bible alone is the religion of protestants."

---

* *Ill News*, 4 *Mass. Hist. Coll.*, II., 19, 20.

These Seekers, Mr. Arnold says in his history of
Rhode Island,* "were afterwards merged in the Society
of Friends," a denomination of Christians which took its
rise about the middle of the seventeenth century. One
of their earliest historians† gives a similar explanation
of the origin of this Society in England; its members, he
says, were there first called Seekers and afterwards
Quakers, but they subsequently assumed the name of
Friends. It was about the year 1648 that the celebrated
George Fox began to publish in England his peculiar
tenets. When he and his followers came to Rhode
Island "they found their brethren already here." Mr.
Callender observes‡ that "the opinions and circumstances
of the people here gave them a very large harvest."
The members of this society became numerous, and
before the close of the first century, they were, we are
told, the most influential denomination in the State.§

It may be proper to add that, from the memorable discussion he had with them in 1672, it is abundantly evident that Roger Williams never embraced the sentiments
of this people. He continued to be a Seeker, to believe
in a visible church, but he expected a new dispensation
to reinaugurate it. Though he never after leaving the
Baptists reunited himself to them, he nevertheless maintained even to the close of his life, that they were the
nearest to the divine original. We have two explicit
declarations of his, giving his belief on the constitution
of the church, and on the form and subjects of baptism.
When an old man, in 1676, he thus expresses himself: ‖

---

* Vol. I. 151.

† William Sewel, *History of the people called Quakers*, p. 6.

‡ *Hist. Disc.*, p. 118.; Ross, *Hist. Disc.*, Newport, 1838, p. 131.

§ Dr. McSparran thus writes in 1752: "In Rhode Island no religion is established, Here a
man may, with impunity, be of any society or none at all; but the Quakers are, for the most
part, the people in power. As Quakerism broke out first in England in 1651, so in 1654, emis-
saries of that enthusiasm were dispatched to the West Indies; and no sooner did their preachers
appear in Rhode Island, but they found many of the posterity of the first planters too well disposed for the reception of that pestilent heresy." *America Dissected.* Updike, *Narragansett
Church*, p. 510.

‖ *George Fox digged out of his Burrowes*, Nar. Club Pub., V. 103.

4

"After all my search and examinations, and considera·
tions, I do profess to believe that some come nearer to
the first primitive churches, and the institutions and
appointments of Christ Jesus than others ; as in many
respects, so in that gallant and heavenly and fundamental
principle of the true matter of a Christian congregation,
flock, or society, viz.: actual believers, tiue disciples and
converts, living stones, such as can give some account how
the grace of God hath appeared unto them and wrought
that heavenly change in them." In a letter* bearing
date 1649, he says : "At Seekonk a great many have
lately concurred with Mr. John Clarke and our Providence men about the point of a new baptism and manner
by dipping, and Mr. John Clarke hath been there lately,
and Mr. Lucar, and hath dipped them. I believe their
practice comes nearer to the first practice of our great
Founder Christ Jesus, than other practices of religion
do."

Before this controversy had subsided, another arose in
the ranks of those holding to a visible church. It re-
ferred to the proper basis of a Christian church, to what
principles entered into the foundation of a true church of
Christ and are essential to its completeness. While some
in the Colony were pushing their principles to the extreme
of doing away with the visible, organized church,
denying the obligations of baptism and the Lord's
Supper, claiming that these have only a spiritual meaning, others were disposed to add to these ordinances
another, the imposition of hands, as an indispensable
prerequisite to church membership and a place at the
memorial feast, citing as authority the words in Hebrews
vi. 1, 2.

The opinion seems to have been first broached both at
Providence and at Newport about the year 1652 ; but
the discussion which followed did not produce a division
in the churches until a few years later, in Providence in

1653-54, and in Newport in 1656.* Dr. Hague relates, on the authority of Mr. Comer, that William Vaughan, of Newport, having learned that a church had been formed at Providence which embraced this tenet and made it a term of communion, repaired thither to pass under the hands of the pastor, Rev. William Wickenden, and that on his return he and others united in forming a similar body at Newport.† This controversy thus rent asunder the Baptist brotherhood of the State. The two parties were rigidly separated from each other ; those holding to the necessity of laying hands upon all church members refused to fellowship such as denied this to be an ordinance of Christ.‡

Five years after he had left the Providence church Roger Williams published his Bloudy Tenent, in which he refers to the classic passage in Hebrews as enunciating the foundation principles of an organized Christian church. It has indeed been affirmed that " he was the first in this country, if not in Europe, of those who have since been Six Principle Baptists, who hold the imposition of hands to be as essential as baptism for any church fellowship." § His conclusion doubtless influenced many in the Colony. When he himself first embraced it, does not appear. While holding this one article, in common with the Six Principle Baptists, in other points quite as essential he differed from them. In belief, we think he came nearer to the Baptists of Pennsylvania and New Jersey. With all his apparent unsettledness in religious matters, it deserves to be men-

---

* " Mr. Samuel Hubbard informs us," says Backus, " that in 1652 the practice was adopted first at Providence and then at Newport." *History*, II. 4. Hubbard was a contemporary of Williams and Clarke, of Wickenden and Vaughan, narrating what took place in his own life-time. Callender remarks further: "About the year 1653 or '54 there was a division in the Baptist church at Providence." " In 1652 some of the brethren at Newport embraced the opinion of laying on of hands ; in 1654 or '56 some withdrew and formed themselves into a church." *Hist. Disc.* pp. 114, 118.

† *Hist. Dist.* p. 97.

‡ Knight, *History Six Principle Baptists*, p. 100.

§ *Nar. Club Pub.*, IV. 21 ; Cf. III. 65.

tioned that he seems never to have been unsettled in his doctrinal views. He was himself a Calvinist, and characterized the opposite system as "that Arminian Popish doctrine of Freewill."* According to their historian, Knight, the Six Principle Baptists of Rhode Island were emphatically Arminian in doctrine. Such, says Callender,† became the church in Providence that "was distinguished by holding laying on of hands necessary to all baptized persons." And the new church in Newport was a protest against Calvinism as well as against indifference in regard to the laying on of hands.‡

The division in Rhode Island was a counterpart of that which took place in England, separating the Baptists into two bodies, the Particular and the General. Crosby, in his history of the English Baptists § observes, "that there have been two parties of the Baptists in England ever since the beginning of the Reformation; those who followed the Calvinistic scheme of doctrines, and from the principal point therein—Personal Election, have been termed Particular Baptists; and those who have professed the Arminian or remonstrant tenets, and have also from the chief of these doctrines—universal redemption, been called General Baptists." The imposition of hands was practised somewhat by both bodies, but not universally by either, though more extensively by the latter than by the former. In this country the Particular Baptists of Pennsylvania held originally to the practice, and the General (or, as they are now more commonly called, the Six Principle) Baptists of Rhode Island, held the same very rigidly. We think there is a deeper significance in these doctrinal differences than at first appears.

---

* *Nar. Club Pub.*, III. 258.

† *Hist. Disc.* p. 115. Benedict, *History*, 1813, I. 486, 487.

‡ "These seceders objected against the old body, *First*—Her use of psalmody. *Second*—Undue restraint upon the liberty of prophesying, as they called it. *Third*—Particular redemption. *Fourth*—Her holding the laying on of hands as a matter of indifference. This last article is supposed to have been the principal cause of the separation." Benedict, I. 500.

§ Vol. I. 173 ; Neal, *History of the Puritans*, II. 110-113.

Among the Particular Baptists of the State still another controversy arose, less extensive in its immediate influence. It was in regard to the Christian Sabbath. There were those who urged that in the substitution of the first day of the week for the seventh, there was a departure from Scripture teaching. The discussion began in 1665, but did not issue in a separate organization until 1671.* As one result of the agitation, two Sabbatarian churches were formed, one at Newport and another in the southwestern part of the State, at Westerly.†

As has been already intimated, the earliest Baptists of the State were strong Calvinists, holding "strictly to the doctrines of sovereign grace." ‡ But later writers speak of a decadence of these views, of doctrinal darkness in some of the churches, of the growth of Arminianism. The falling off of the Six Principle churches was in part on doctrinal grounds, they embracing the tenets of the General Baptists. And in the other churches there may have been a modification of the doctrines formerly held, or rather an expansion and fuller explication of them. They did not, it would seem, forsake the "doctrines of grace," but learned that they could with consistency maintain the general provisions of the gospel, while insisting as strongly as ever on their particular application. For, in the langnge of Dr. Archibald Alexander, "the cardinal point of difference between Calvinists and Arminians is, whether the reason

---

*First Newport Church records; Backus, I. 325; Arnold II. 36.

† Thus early, shortly after the settlement of the State, four denominations of Christians had appeared, three of which took their origin in this period, in the very controversies we have noticed. Of the Friends it has been said that as "a body of Christians it took its rise in England about the middle of the seventeenth century." Of the Sabbatarians: "There were likely two congregations of the Sabbatarians iu London ; one among the General Baptists, meeting in Mill Yard, the trust-deeds of which date as far back as 1678 ; the other the Particular Baptists, in Cripplegate." Encyclopedia of Religious Knowledge. The earliest Episcopal church within the Colony was organized in 1699 ; and the first Congregational in 1720. Other denominations came later. A church was gathered in 1783 on an independent basis, which subsequently united with the Freewill Baptists, the first of this name in the Colony. The first church of this denomination in North America was formed only three years earlier, in 1780, nearly a century and a half after the settlement of the State. Ency. Relig. Knowl.

‡ Backus, II. 2.

why one man is saved and another not, is owing to the grace of God, or to the free will of man." Judged by this standard we think there was very little Arminianism in the Baptist churches of New England outside of the Six Principle body for the first hundred years. Dr. Neale well says : * "This charge from the lips of those in sympathy with Dr. Gill requires considerable abatement." At a somewhat later period there were individual cases of doctrinal defection, a few persons becoming imbued even with Socinianism. Spiritual life was, however, very feeble, the churches partaking of the general apathy that rested like a pall upon all the New England colonies. The general deadness arrested the attention of the more devout and led them to plead in special prayer for a revival of religion. The coming to these shores of that earnest and singularly gifted man, George Whitfield, in 1740, was followed by one of the most wonderful awakenings in the history of the church. All New England felt the stimulating effect. One of its marked features was the multiplying of Baptist churches in Massachusetts and Connecticut † and the quickening of religious life in Rhode Island. These "Separatists," or "New Lights," as those Baptists were called who had come out from the "standing order," visited by invitation the "old Baptists" of the Narragansett country with most gratifying results. Spiritual life and

---

* *Hist. Disc.*, Boston, 1865, p. 25.

† For an interesting account of this multiplication of Baptist churches. see *Historical Discourse* by David Weston, Middleborough, 1868, entitled *The Baptist Movement of a Hundred Years Ago, and its Vindication*. The author calls attention to the fact that a similar phenomenon has been often witnessed in the history of the church. He says, " Trace back the record of church history to the early centuries, and it will be invariably found that every time of quickening and reformation has produced Baptists." " The Great Reformation of the sixteenth century could never have occurred if it had not been heralded by Baptists." Pp. 15, 16.

" At this time (1549) there were many Anabaptists in several parts of England. They were generally Germans, whom the revolutions there had forced to change their seats. Upon Luther's first preaching in Germany there arose many, who building on some of his principles, carried things much further than he did. The chief foundation he laid was, that the Scripture was the only rule of Christians." Burnet, *History of the Reformation*, 4th ed., London, 1715, pt. II. bk. I. Vol. II. 105. Luther was indeed strenuously opposed on the very ground that his principles, if consistently followed, would conduct him to the position maintained by the Anabaptists.

activity appeared. Churches that had affiliated with the Six Principle Baptists were dissolving this connection. Changes elsewhere were also taking place. The Providence church was turning toward the doctrinal views of the first settlers of the Colony and was at the same time relaxing its former strictness in regard to the laying on of hands. As early as 1730, Governor Jenckes, a member of this church, wrote to his pastor concurring in the opinion that the neglect of this rite "should be no bar to communion with those who have been rightly baptized."* At the beginning of President Manning's ministry, it was by a vote of the church set aside as a term of communion,† not, however, as an ordinance of Christ for the sake of union with other Christians, but because it had ceased to be regarded as such an ordinance; this conclusion reached, the custom fell into desuetude. And in Newport, immediately after the death of the pastor, Rev. Gardner Thurston, which occurred in 1802, the Second church, having been prepared for it during the latter part of his ministry, made a change in its ecclesiastical relations. This church, says Mr. Knight in his history,‡ who wrote as an eye-witness, "appear to have rather swerved from their ancient faith and practice." The church had reached the doctrinal position of the regular Baptists. That remarkable revival of living

---

" The Rev. Archbishop Whitgift, and the learned Hooker, men of great judgment and famous in their time, did long since foresee, and accordingly declared their fear that if ever Puritanism should prevail among us, it would soon draw in Anabaptism after it. At this Cartwright and others, the advocates for the Disciplinarian interest in those days, seemed to take great offence. But these good men judged right. They only considered, as prudent men, that Anabaptism had its rise from the same principles the Puritans held, and its growth, from the same courses they took; together with the natural tendency of their principles and practices thitherward; especially that one principle, as it was by them understood, that the Scripture was *adequata agendorum regula*, so as nothing might be lawfully done without express warrant either from some command or example therein contained. The clue thereof, if followed on as far as it would lead, would certainly in time carry them as far as the Anabaptists were then gone." Bishop Sanderson, *Sermons*, London, 1681, preface §XXIII.

* Guild, *Manning and Brown University*, p. 153.

† Hague, p. 107; Backus, II. 493.

‡ Page 262. And Backus says, "The doctrines of grace gradually gained ground in this church." *History*, II. 500.

piety which swept with blessed influences over the New
England states and, extending beyond them, aroused the
slumbering churches, was indeed a revival also of Calvinism in the churches, the Calvinism of Andrew Fuller,
however, rather than that of John Gill. The doctrines
of grace, which had become sadly obscured among the
Congregationalists of Massachusetts and the General Baptists of Rhode Island, were made to stand forth in their
beauty and power during the great Awakening. The preva-
lent type of piety was considerably modified. Religious
life became less introspective and more outward, more
aggressive, more missionary. A new era was about to
dawn, an era of growth and rapid multiplication. With
these changes, new wants were developed ; and there
was a feeling after fellowship, sympathy, coöperation,—
toward a completer recognition of the mutual relation of
churches.

THE ASSOCIATION OF CHURCHES—ORGANIC UNITY.

We now reach the period when the oldest of our New
England associations was formed, the year 1767. For
the next fifty years and more, the history of this Association is well nigh the history of the denomination in
the State. The principle was not a new one, as sometimes
represented. The Philadelphia Association had already
been sixty years in existence, having been organized in
1707. Other associations had been formed in the more
Southern States.* Nor were the New England churches
wholly unacquainted with such voluntary bodies. The
Six Principle churches had, according to Knight, since
"about the close of the sixteenth (meaning the seventeenth") century, united in a yearly meeting composed
of elders, messengers," &c.† And the Calvinistic churches

* There were already five associations at the South. "The Ketochton Association was
formed in 1766, and was the fifth association of the Calvinistic Baptists in America. The Philadelphia, the Charleston, Sandy Creek and Kehukee Associations were formed before it." Benedict, *History*, II. 34.

† *History*, p. 322. Caldwell, *Centennial Discourse*, Warren Assoc., 1867, p. 29.

had early contemplated the formation of a similar body, as appears from the following record made in 1734 :* "Had some discourse about coming into an association with the churches of our communion, to which no one made any objection or showed any reluctance, but all that spoke seemed to approve the scheme and to desire to guard against the disorders that have attended some General Meetings." Besides the considerations influential in 1734, many others were potent in 1767. It was a transition period with some churches and more individuals. Baptist churches had multiplied in Massachusetts, and the Six Principle yearly meeting had greatly declined, if it had not already ceased to exist. The churches that were essentially one in doctrine and practice, demanded some recognized bond of union, some expression of their common life. Work was, moreover, thrust upon them which could be effectually done only by combination. Baptists in the neighboring states needed moral support and protection against unjust laws. And the infant college required the fostering care of the Baptists of this section, as well as of Pennsylvania and the South.

Thus we discover preparations for the Association formed at Warren. But the task óf bringing together and unifying the different elements of which it was to be composed, was slowly accomplished. The proposed association was to embrace the few original Calvinistic churches, such Six Principle churches as had become Calvinistic in doctrine and had ceased to regard the imposition of hands as an ordinance of Christ, and the Baptist churches that had arisen out of the Separatist movement, especially in Massachusetts. These several classes of churches, though virtually one in faith and practice, were evidently somewhat afraid of each other, and naturally shy of committing themselves to an enter-

* *First Newport Church records.*

prise that might endanger the truth, or abridge their liberties. And, too, not a few Baptists had suffered so much from synods, and councils, and clerical associations in Massachusetts and Connecticut, that for this reason also they moved in the matter with extreme caution.* Similar difficulties were encountered in Virginia when the Regulars and Separates of that State were merged into one body on the basis of a common confession.† In illustrating this principle—the association of churches—from the Warren Association, we shall briefly pass under review its basis of union, the powers it claimed, and the purpose it contemplated.

The first step taken in organizing the Association was to form *a basis of union*. Its projectors thought, and thought wisely, that for the union to be pleasant and effective, or even possible for the ends sought, all the churches coming into the body must stand upon the same platform ; have substantially the same belief and agree in church order ; in other words, they must have a common understanding of the teachings of the Word of God, both as to what it is to be a Christian, and what constitutes a church. As it drew its inspiration from Philadelphia, so the Association organized after the model Philadelphia had shown. It rested upon the same basis. The Philadelphia Association had in 1746 declared that "churches ought to unite in faith and practice, and to have and maintain communion together, in order to associate regularly, because the latter is founded upon and arises from the former." That Association was composed of churches Calvinistic in doctrine, Congregational in government, and restricted in fellowship. A like body was contemplated by the Warren church, of which President Manning was then the pastor, when it voted ‡ that "an association be entered into with sundry churches of the same faith and order." When the appointed delegates from the churches came together, on the eighth of September, 1767, "the issue of the meeting was, adopting the sentiments and platform of the Western (Philadelphia) Association, and thereon forming themselves into a like body to be known as the Warren Association." Two years later the platform was slightly modified, and then, the same year, 1769, it was printed with a prefatory note containing the declaration given above, that on the platform of the Western Association the delegates at Warren formed themselves into a like body.* The Philadelphia Association recognized the likeness, addressing its first letter "to the elders and messengers of the several Baptist churches of the same faith and order, to meet in association at Warren." The platform further states the manner and conditions of admission into the body as follows : "Churches are to be received into this Association by petitions setting forth their desire to be admitted, their faith, order, and willingness to be conformable to the rules of the associated body." Thus it is evident that the basis of union provides for a homogeneous body, a body composed of churches in substantial agreement, seeing eye to eye, having the same belief as to the way of salvation and the method of church building.

We proceed to inquire *what powers* were claimed and exercised by the Association? The Association was not a synod, nor a presbytery, nor a classis, nor in any sense a court of judicature, and could not exercise the powers of such bodies. It had nothing whatever to do with churches not belonging to it, and nothing at all with the internal affairs of churches connected with it. It sacredly abstained from laying its hands upon the independence of the individual churches. It was emphatic in "dis-

---

* This was printed on a separate sheet ; a copy of which is bound up with a complete list of the minutes of the Association, in the library of Brown University. This platform appears entire in Guild's *Manning*, 73-39 ; Backus, II. 413.

claiming superiority, jurisdiction, coercive right, and in-
fallibility," assuming to be "no other than an advisory
council." It was a voluntary body, that is, a body
which the different members, the individual churches,
had voluntarily entered, and it claimed the powers—no
more, no less—of other like bodies, voluntary associations. As such it claimed the right to frame its own
constitution, to make its own by-laws, to determine the
conditions of membership, to enforce its own rules, and
to preserve its own integrity ; its rules and regulations,
however, to be always conformable to Scripture. Like
the churches of which it was composed, it was an independent body under Christ. It was under no obligation
to receive a church because it applied for admission, nor
to retain one when admitted if it depart from its faith
and violate the original compact. In dissolving its connection with a constituent, its course was determined by
no outside body called to sit in judgment upon its acts.
It asked permission of no one to strike a church from its
roll of members.

These statements are confirmed by the history of the
Association. It has from the beginning examined all
applicants by a committee "on the admission of new
churches." This examination, provided for in the original basis of union, and observed through all the subsequent years, implies a standard, and the right both to
reject applicants not conforming to it, and to cut off any
member of the body departing therefrom. From the
minutes of the Association, we learn that it has during
its history dropped several churches, because they failed
to comply with the conditions of admission. Mr. Backus,
who was the first clerk of the Warren Association, and
prominent during all its earlier years, having indeed
much to do in shaping its policy, and who knows therefore whereof he affirms, says of this and similar bodies,
"that they refuse to hear and judge of any personal
controversy in any of their churches, or to intermeddle

with the affairs of any church which hath not freely joined with them." He adds in regard to their own churches: "If any church refuse to report its condition annually to the association, or if the church departs from her former faith and order, she is left out of the association." * These quotations are explicit and require no comments. The right to protect itself, to excind unworthy members, was both claimed and exercised. Churches were sometimes, indeed, even while still members, forbidden by vote from taking seats in the body, when cause was shown.† Nor was there ever any complaint that church independency was thereby infringed.

The powers claimed will still further appear if we consider *the purpose* for which the Association was organized. This was three-fold. First, to give expression to an already existing fact, the essential oneness of their churches, to make visible the truth of this agreement in faith and practice and their consequent fellowship. Although their local churches were not parts of an organized whole, but were independent bodies, each complete in itself, yet they were not Ishmaelitish, acknowledging no peculiar relationship and obligation, but were essentially one in the truth. And they would by means of association form a bond in recognition of the union, one that should at the same time draw them closer together for mutual protection and aggressive work.

A second purpose of the Association was to preserve the unity and doctrinal purity of the churches ; to maintain the New Testament faith and order, to defend the integrity of the truth, and to build churches after the model the apostles furnished. This purpose was incorporated into the platform, wherein it is declared that "some of the uses of it (the Association) are union and commun-

---

*Backus, II. 413. See also a discussion of *The Mutual Relation of Baptist Churches,* by Rev. W. H. H. Marsh, *Baptist Quarterly,* October, 1874.

† *Minutes* for 1788.

ion among themselves; maintaining more effectually the faith delivered to the saints, having advice in cases of doubt, and help in distress, being more able to promote the good of the cause." In the circular letter of 1768, the writer * expressed joy that "so many churches were willing to promote union and fellowship, and contend earnestly for the faith once delivered to the saints." The same intent appears in the constitutional provisions for the admission of churches and in the uniform practice of the Association through its entire history, namely, to examine all applicants as to "their faith and order." Even in the dismission of churches this aim was made manifest. For instance, in 1808 it was voted that if certain churches "from their local situation should find it more convenient to join other associations of the same faith and order, they are at liberty so to do; only they give us suitable notice of their proceedings." The churches were reminded of their duties to the Association, which insisted upon its rights. On one occasion † it dismissed a church, which had somewhat unceremoniously severed itself from the body, with this gentle rebuke, "though asking our previous advice might have been more expedient."

The doctrinal views of the Association, in the first instance declared to be set forth in the Confession of 1689 as adopted by the Philadelphia Association, were often and emphatically expressed, especially during the early history of the body. Queries both doctrinal and practical were frequently submitted and replies given; and, if space permitted, it would be interesting and instructive to reproduce some of these questions and answers.‡

---

* Dr. Stillman.

† In 1783.

‡ For example, in 1782, "The church at Harwich having requested advice as to the best mode of proceeding in case any church should deviate from the faith and order of the gospel as held by these churches. Voted: We are of opinion that in such case the neighboring churches ought to inform the deviating church of their uneasiness, and desire a candid hearing; if this is denied, or, if it be granted, and satisfaction is not obtained, they should withdraw fellowship from said church, and give information at the Association, who have a right to drop such church from this body." See also minutes for 1793, 1799, 1802, 1803, 1809, 1820.

That the Association jealously guarded against the approaches of error, and sought to conserve the doctrinal purity of the churches is abundantly evident.

The following item is from the minutes of 1784 : "As it is a time of the prevalence of error of every kind, and of the apostacy of many from the faith of the gospel, it is recommended to the churches, that they express in their annual letters to the Association, their particular adherence to the doctrines of grace."

The carefulness evinced in regard to the character of its own members was extended also to that of its affiliated bodies. A perusal of the minutes of the Association shows that its procedure was precisely the same with bodies seeking correspondence as with churches applying for membership. The faith and order required in the one case were required also in the other. The same tests of fellowship were applied to both. Provision was made at the very outset for "a connection to be formed and maintained between this Association and that of Philadelphia, by annual letter and messengers from us to them and from them to us." This was the beginning of a wide correspondence with similar bodies organized in different sections of the country. Whenever a kindred organization expressed a desire to open such correspondence, inquiry was invariably made into the belief and practice of the applicant, and if these were satisfactory, the request was granted and it was taken "into union and fellowship." We will cite two instances by way of illustrating the method of the Association when such applications were made. An association in New Hampshire was represented in the session of 1784, and gave, the records say, "a clear and satisfactory account of their faith and order," and "they were received into brotherly connection with us." Again in 1801, the Leyden Association appeared by its representatives, "to open" in the language of the original minutes, "a correspondence with us ; after obtaining satisfaction respecting their faith and order, voted to receive them into our connection." The following are some of the oft-recurring phrases used when associations were admitted to correspondence:—"received into brotherly connection with us,"—"into union with us,"—"into fellowship and connection with us." A single exception confirms the rule. The Groton Conference, though composed of churches practising mixed communion, was, in 1798, taken into correspondence ; but the departure from the phraseology used on similar occasions, is significant. The records say that upon the reading of the letter, it was "Voted to send messengers to the Groton Conference agreeably to their request, hoping it may be a means of promoting Christian candor and mutual advantage." There must have been something in the condition of these churches to encourage the expectation that this course would promote the cause of truth and lead to cordial fellowship. It is a matter of history that these churches subsequently embraced restricted communion views.*

The third purpose of the Association was to stimulate the churches and combine them for more effective aggressive work. What could not be done or even attempted by any single church, might be accomplished by the

---

* Many familiar only with the present practice of the Association, may, after reading the preceeding pages, inquire how the character of the Association's correspondence has been so radically changed. For a period of eighty-one years, until 1848, it maintained its correspondence as originally established, with bodies of "the same faith and order." In 1849, without giving any reason so far as the records show, it omitted to appoint its customary delegates, and never resumed the custom ; but the annual "Committtee on Minutes of Corresponding Bodies," was continued.

At the session of 1858, this Committee on Correspondence reported that no minutes had been received, and took the liberty through the Moderator to introduce the President and Clerk of the Freewill Baptist Conference of Rhode Island. After addresses by these brethren, it was "Voted, that three delegates be appointed to attend the annual meeting of the Rhode Island Conference of Freewill Baptists at Olneyville, next June." Delegates were also appointed to meet with the Six Principle Baptists, and, at a subsequent stage of the same meeting, to the Seventh Day Baptists. This is the first time in the course of the Association's history that such appointments were made. The next year delegates were again sent; and the year following, 1860, a committee "was appointed to nominate delegates to corresponding bodies." Thus, the second year after the innovation was made, these several bodies were designated "corresponding bodies," the term being evidently used in an entirely new sense. In 1862 the Congregationalists were included in the number of corresponding bodies, and a little later the Methodists.

churches in organized combination. Many of the churches in Massachusetts, suffering from the ecclesiastical laws of the State, needed such assistance as could be rendered only by the churches acting in concert. Thus combining, they would "be more able to promote the good of the cause," and "become more important in the eye of civil powers." The Association made itself felt by the General Court at Boston, and in connection with other similar bodies by the Continental Congress. To obtain relief for distressed brethren was one of the first duties with which it charged itself. For ten years Isaac Backus continued most faithfully to serve the Association as its agent, to secure for his brethren exemption from civil liabilities for their religious opinions, and, if possible, the repeal of all odious laws against the "sectaries." These labors in behalf of religious liberty, which were ultimately crowned with signal success, form an honorable chapter in Baptist history.*

While making these heroic efforts for brethren harassed and oppressed with cruel burdens, and nobly seeking the dissemination of more liberal ideas and broader principles, the men who projected the Association were also diligently strengthening the foundations of the college that was to become the pride of the State and a source of power to the denomination. The sentiments entertained by the founders of the State concerning the value and importance of education are most honorable to them, and their endeavors to promote it worthy of all praise.

* For a full account of these struggles and triumphs, see Dr. Hovey's *Life and Times of Isaac Backus;* a book that should be carefully read, especially by every Baptist. Both at the settlement of the colonies and at the period of the Revolution, Baptists were permitted to bear a conspicuous part in securing liberty to the American people. And it is an interesting fact that the Baptist church served as a model for the national government. "There was a small Baptist church, which held its monthly meetings for business at a short distance from Mr. Jefferson's house, eight or ten years before the American Revolution. Mr. Jefferson attended these meetings for several months in succession. The pastor on one occasion asked him how he was pleased with the church government? Mr. Jefferson replied that it struck him with great force, and had interested him much ; *that he considered it the only form of true democracy then existing in the world*, and had concluded that it would be the best plan of government for the American colonies. Curtis, *Progress of Baptist Principles,* p. 356.

Some of the original planters were themselves men of considerable culture. A few Baptists, of a later period, though at a personal sacrifice, availed themselves of provisions secured at Harvard especially for Baptist students through the munificence of Mr. Thomas Hollis, of London. While an encouraging number of generous youths were reaching toward the largest possible attainments in knowledge, a movement was very early made in this State for the education and general enlightenment of the many,—of all the young. By a vote of the town of Newport, August 20, 1640,* Mr. Robert Lenthall "was called to keep a public school for the learning of youth." And an appropriation was made for his support, so that all, even the poorest, children might avail themselves of its advantages. It is claimed, and perhaps the claim is not ill-founded, that Rhode Island may boast of having had the first free school in America;† and a Baptist had the honor of being the first public school teacher.‡

As to the question of an educated ministry, our fathers never entertained the opinion that none but thoroughly trained men were fit to be inducted into the sacred office ; much less did they commit the fatal mistake of substituting culture for piety in their spiritual guides. With them the teaching of the schools was no compensation for the teaching of the Spirit. They preferred indeed the "lowly preaching" of the godly to the polished discourses of the unregenerate. While strongly pro-

---

* *Newport Town Records ;* Callender, p. 116; Arnold, I. 145.

† The writer is indebted to the Hon. Wm. P. Sheffield, of Newport, for calling his attention to the fact that this movement for public schools antedated similar action by any other colony. Although Harvard College was founded in 1638, to provide a learned ministry for the churches, public schools, controlled and maintained by the government for the public good, were not attempted by the Massachusetts Colony until 1647, *Mass. Col. Rec.*, II. 203, nor by the Plymouth colony until 1770, *Ply. Col. Rec.*, V., 107 ; see also Baylies' *Memoirs of Ply. Col.*, Vol. 1. pt. i., 241; pt. ii., 67, 93. Yet Gov. Bradford early conceived the idea of giving instruction to the young of his Colony, but encountered insuperable difficulties, *Hist. Ply. Plantation ;* 4 *Mass. Hist. Coll.*, III. 161; Cf. Bacon's *Genesis of the New. Eng. Churches*, p. 397.

‡ Winthrop, I. 287, 288 ; Hubbard, 2 *Mass. Hist. Coll.*, V. 275 ; Backus, I. 97 ; Caldwell, *Hist. Disc.*, p. 27. Lenthall was admitted a freeman at Newport in 1640, *R. I. Col. Rec.*, I., 104.

testing against a prevailing evil of the times, admitting
into the pulpit ungodly men because. they had been
taught in the schools with a view to the clerical profession,—against the pernicious custom of making education instead of piety, the indispensable qualification
for the ministry, they nevertheless believed—the leaders
at any rate—that genuine piety was none the worse for
being conjoined with true culture, that a godly ministry
would be all the more efficient for being disciplined and
taught. At the earliest practicable moment a Baptist
college, or, more properly, a college to be under Baptist
control, was established at Providence, where Baptist
youth might have equal advantages with other students,
—"wherein education might be promoted, and superior
learning obtained, free of any sectarian religious tests."*
This stands seventh in the list of American colleges.†
First proposed by the Baptists of Pennsylvania and New
Jersey, it received during its earlier years generous con-
tributions from the South as well as from the churches
of Massachusetts and Rhode Island.‡

In connection with the Association, other enterprises
were successively inaugurated. The principle of combination was applied to missionary projects, to the assistance of young men preparing for the ministry, to the
evangelization of the uncultivated portions of the State,
to the carrying of the gospel to the heathen. But we
cannot enlarge upon these points; it must suffice merely
to state that the principle of association has been variously
applied. One item, however, from the minutes of the
Association for 1822 may be of interest. "Read the
articles adopted by the South Carolina State Baptist
Convention; whereupon Resolved, that this Association
cheerfully accord with the principles adopted by that

---

* Backus, II. 137.

† Those preceding it were founded in the following order : Harvard (Cong.), 1638; William
and Mary (Epis.), 1692; Yale (Cong.), 1701; Princeton (Presb.), 1746 ; University of Pennsylvania (Epis.), 1753 ; Columbia (Epis.), 1754.

‡ *Warren Assoc. Minutes*, 1774; Backus, II. 494.

body, and that we cordially unite with our brethren in the formation of a similar institution." Three years later the Missionary Convention was formed whose Jubilee we to-day celebrate.

Having overcome their first fears, our fathers learned to prize the principle of association. They expressed it as their conviction in 1809 that great good resulted "from the union of our churches into associations, and the reciprocal communications of associations with each other. The benefits of these correspondencies have been already experienced in a pleasing and profitable degree, and we conceive they may be more extensively experienced by a more full and mature cultivation of the plan." Indeed, the advantages thence arising were so thoroughly appreciated, and the principle was believed to be so accordant with Scripture teaching, that many would carry the principle still further and bring into a kind of organic union the Baptist brotherhood of the United States. The idea was more than suggested in the first letter of the Philadelphia Association :* "A long course of experience and observation, "they say," has taught us to have the highest sense of the advantages which accrue from association ; nor, indeed, does the nature of the thing speak any other language. For, as particular members are collected together and united in one body, which we call a particular church, to answer those ends and purposes which could not be accomplished by any single member, so a collection and union into one associational body may easily be conceived capable of answering those still greater purposes which any particular church could not be equal to. And, by the same reason, a union of associations will still increase the body in weight and strength, and make it good that a threefold cord of strength is not easily broken." Several unsuccessful attempts were made to realize this idea of organic unity. In 1828 the Warren Association

* Contained in Guild's *Manning*, pp. 76, 77.

concurred in the opinion "That the time has arrived when we should have some regularly constituted bond or centre of union toward which, as a denomination, we might look." It was recommended that "the Baptist General Convention for Missionary Purposes take into consideration the propriety of forming an American Baptist Convention, to assemble triennially in a central part of the United States." These attempts, though perhaps impracticable, show conclusively that, so far from fearing the centralizing influence of associations, lest they should undermine the independence of the churches, many among the fathers were disposed to make the associations serve a still further purpose—to bind the denomination into an organized whole, or rather, to give expression to the existing fact of its essential oneness and homogeneity.*

We have thus passed under review some of the distinctive principles of the Baptists, imperfectly it must be confessed, but with sufficient fullness, it is hoped, to leave no doubt as to the historical attitude of the denomination in the State. The churches did not push their ideas of liberty to the confines of license, nor their notions of church independence to the extreme of isolation. The fathers believed that the churches, though independent, should associate themselves together, but that, while free to manage their own internal affairs, they had no right to modify their faith and practice and still claim to remain in associational connection. There is a definite body of

---

* These efforts for organic unity furnish an interesting study. The attempt to realize the idea was made by a General Committee, *Minutes* for 1791 and 1793 ; also by a General Association, or Convention. Possibly we have not made enough of our associations. Perhaps the principle of church independency has been lifted so high as quite to overshadow, if not entirely to conceal, another equally important principle, namely, the fellowship of the churches and their mutual relation. " The two foci of our ellipse are, on the one side, the independence of the local church and, on the other, the mutual friendship and helpful co-working of all local churches." Dexter, *Congregationalism*, p. 299. This early movement toward organic unity may profitably be compared with that recently made by our German brethren, which has resulted in the Baptist "Bund." Compare also the movement made for the unification of the Presbyterians under the lead of Dr. McCosh.

principles which our churches have held with almost uniform consistency from the very beginning. Oneness of doctrine and discipline has been a condition of denominational fellowship.

If we would trace our principles in their wide-spread growth and to their remoter influences, we must pass beyond our own communion into other religious societies, among Christians of other names. For many of the principles for which our fathers were contending a century, and even a half-century ago, and for holding which they suffered fines and imprisonments, are now the accepted faith of Christendom. They have become the common possession of the religious world—have entered into the thinking of the age. They would no more be questioned to-day than the movements of the earth around the sun, or the constant force of gravitation. And, but for the testimony of history, it would be difficult to believe that they were ever subjects of bitter controversy and their adherents cruelly persecuted.

Other principles, however, scarcely less important, and intimately related to the advancement of the Redeemer's kingdom on earth, are still in litigation. But, even in regard to these, a change of front is presented. The old issues are indeed dead, but new ones are constantly arising. The conflicts of the church are not all past. She is even now engaged in a triangular warfare. There are, on the one hand, tendencies toward laxity of doctrinal views,—to put a low estimate upon principles, to esteem all opinions equally good if held with equal honesty; our very liberty may degenerate into latitudinarianism. And there are, on the other hand, tendencies in the direction of the substitution of forms for simple faith in Christ,—to invest the ordinances of the church with sacramental efficacy. The baptismal controversy, for example, is not simply a question about the *form* of a rite, though this were not unimportant if it involves obedience to the head of the church; nor is it merely a

question respecting the proper *subjects* of the rite, though
this embraces the very constitution of the church Christ
established. The controversy touches still deeper than
this, and concerns the *office* of the rite, what it does for
him who submits to it, whether indeed it be a regenerat-
ing act, by which, for example, an unconscious child is
made the fitter for heaven, or an unrepentant sinner is
put in possession of the Holy Spirit,—involving thus the
most essential doctrines of the gospel.* So long as this
question remains an open one the work of the denomination will not be done, nor will it be at liberty to resign
its trust.

For the further prosecution of its work the denomination may gather inspiration from its history. The
wonderful growth of our principles in the past is a bright
prophecy respecting their future progress, as regards both
the numbers that shall embrace them and the clearness
with which they shall be apprehended. But all true progress it is well to remind ourselves, is toward the Scriptures, toward a better understanding of them and a
wider application of their truths. Science with all her
boasted progress within the last half century—and it has
been marvellous—has added not one law nor a single new
force to the realm of nature; her progress has been
toward a clearer apprehension and a fitter classification of
the laws and forces that have been from the beginning.
In like manner, progress in religious knowledge consists
not in leaving the Bible, nor in supplementing its con-
tents, but in obtaining constantly broader views and a
stronger grasp of the everlasting truths inlaid in God's
Book. Our principles must be constantly measured by
the unerring teachings of Scripture. And thus by
approaching this infallible standard, the different denominations of Christians will draw closer together, and may
finally become one in the truth. The church of the

* See article on *Present State of the Baptismal Controversy*, by Dr. Hovey, *Baptist Quarterly*, April, 1875.

future will be a reproduction, enlarged and glorified, of the church of the first century ; it will appeal to the same ultimate standard, will embrace the same fundamental principles, and will be animated by the same spirit of self-sacrifice and devotion.

In studying the successes achieved by our fathers we are impressed with two facts, evidently influential with them and contributing to their success, facts which we shall do well to bear in mind.

First, that our principles are GOD'S TRUTHS. They are not uncertain speculations, mere human opinions, but truths divinely revealed, which we are therefore not at liberty to displace or modify, but to preserve in their integrity.

Secondly, that these truths have been committed to us IN TRUST. They are ours to defend and proclaim. The church is the Lord's whose government we are to administer in his name. The ordinances are the Lord's which we are to observe in his own prescribed way. The gospel is indeed itself a sacred trust committed to us to make known to those sitting in darkness and in the shadow of death. May we prove the faithful heralds of salvation, worthy successors of men who counted not their lives dear unto themselves, but were willing to sacrifice their all to maintain the spirituality of the church, the integrity of the ordinances, and the personal nature of religion. Thus true to our doctrines and loyal to our King, we shall toil under his approving smiles and be permitted to hasten the triumphs of his kingdom in the earth.